RIVER WITH NO NAME

A Collection of Poems

Mason Shine

Published by Mason Shine

Copyright © 2024 Mason Shine

All rights reserved

The characters and events portrayed in this book are fictitious. Any similarity to real persons, living or dead, is coincidental and not intended by the author.

No part of this book may be reproduced, or stored in a retrieval system, or transmitted in any form or by any means, electronic, mechanical, photocopying, recording, or otherwise, without express written permission of the publisher.

ISBN: 979-8-9910027-0-7

Cover design by: Dax Hickey
Illustrations by: Dax Hickey

Printed in the United States of America

I'd like to dedicate this book to my wife Danika, who first encouraged me to put these poems together. What started as my attempt to communicate my feelings and struggles to her is now this book in your hand, and it is all thanks to her. Thank you so much Danika for believing in me and my writing.

CONTENTS

Title Page
Copyright
Dedication
I.	1
II.	3
III.	5
IV.	7
V.	11
VI.	13
VII.	15
VIII.	19
IX.	21
X.	23
XI.	25
XII.	27
XIII.	29
XIV.	31
XV.	33

XVI.	35
XVII.	37
XVIII.	39
XIX.	43
XX.	45
XXI.	47
XXII.	51
XXIII.	53
XXIV.	55
XXV.	57
XXVI	59
XXVII.	61
XXVIII.	63
XXIX.	65
XXX.	67
XXXI.	69
XXXII.	71
XXXIII. My Most Precious Daughter	73
XXXIV.	75
XXXV.	77
XXXVI.	79
XXXVII.	81
XXXVIII.	83
XXXIX.	85
XL.	87
XLI.	89

I.

My mind is fog
My tongue concrete
My heart lead
I have nothing to offer.
The words I do have are barbed.
My throat is coated
in blood
I'm tired
of forcing them out.
They have no home,
why subject them
to this cruel reality?
They neither give
or receive refuge.

Silence is safe
for all

* * *

II.

I wish I could open
my mind to you
But first I would have to take your hand
and trudge through the mud,
and greet the skeletons that live there.
We would have to get lost in the desert,
chasing some oasis.
First we would have to embrace
the solitary crowd of thoughts.
Maybe then we could reach
the vault of my fears, would you dare
to open it, if I gave you the code?

The fear that is like reinforced steel
is that you will discover my mind is
the prison of
my
own
making.

If you open it
and peer through the foggy veil
there will be a small door.
Crouch down, go inside.
See the young boy
sitting
crying
alone in his room.

III.

There's a landscape
shrouded in fog and mist
Dark, mysterious, majestic
People admire it, appreciate it
The greys and dark browns
are beautiful
It looks special, but it's a lie
Behind the fog
trees are barren
leaves fallen dead
on the ground
Behind the mist
grass is burnt
weeds have taken over
Behind the mystery
is revealed a chasm
empty, dangerous
Will the people see it?
Before they fall in?

IV.

What's in the chasm?

Nothing.

Nothing? What is the name of the river that carved it?

It's a river with no name.

Name it then,

No.

But why? What is in the chasm? Do you fear it?

Nothing, that is the scariest part. No monsters, no pain, no feeling, no life, nothing to hide. It was eroded by a river that has no name.

I will name it then.

Who can name the water? Is water not life?

So, life created the chasm?

No, the river cannot be named, are we to attribute the chasm to life? Does life not create all things? It is not life's fault.

This is foolish then.

I agree.

So, there is nothing to fear in the chasm?

Yes, but it is the chasm itself that is to be feared.

I will fill it then.

You're new here, it cannot be done. We must acknowledge
it here, deal with it.
The chasm carved,
by the river
with no name.

* * *

V.

I am Jack's isolation
and spiritual despair

I begin the day with bloody knuckles
and a broken nose

I wake up in the blue corner
My shadow is in the red corner

I fight alone

I know all my
weaknesses

I'm an easy opponent.

VI.

Hidden for a while
Underneath my laugh and smile
My darkness is back

VII.

I'm paddling through pudding
A Long Lake of pudding
Seems like a kid's dream
Not mine

It's thick
Slow
Dark
Can't move

I feel like the horse in that movie
The Never Ending Story
Sebastian I think.
Stuck in the mud
He worked hard to get out
But knew it was over

I'm also the wolf
chasing Sebastian and his Atreu
Fast
Vicious
Deadly

Atreu has to make a decision
Stay
Or survive
He survives

Atreu is the people in my life
trying to save me from the mud
They don't know the wolf is close

They care
and they pull on the reigns
but I can't move
can't escape

I'm watching the VHS
wanting Atreu to escape
This movie has to have a good ending

* * *

VIII.

Sometimes,
yes,
I am the talking horse,
from that tv show.
I drift, unblinking,
between scenes

* * *

IX.

I've been eyeing
the rope
in our top drawer.
You know which one,
the black one.
I could use it
and escape my mind,
let down the rope through an ethereal window,
slip out.
I think to myself,
whether to double it
for extra strength
and comfort,
it's what I do for your wrists.
How will it feel
on my skin
instead of yours?
Would it leave the same marks
on my neck,
as on your wrists?

It's shape speaks
of my love for you
and my hate
for me.

X.

I'm paradoxical
I see the beauty
and purpose
of the lives around me,
but fail to grasp my own.
God can forgive and love,
enough for the universe,
but I am too great a weight
to bare.
I am an open ear
that provides comfort,
but am captive by
a mouth, and mind
shut,
unable to receive.

* * *

XI.

My words are written
with tears
and blood,
mixed with sweat.
Yet they are utterly insufficient
in describing my pain.
They are a cloudy, and distant
reflection
of the beauty I have found
in you.
They fall terribly short
when trying to span the distance between
us.
They drowned,
somewhere in the ocean.

                    I'm sorry for that.

* * *

XII.

The crow observes me
a single eye pointed my way,
focused.
I have bread in my hand
and I know he gazes at me.
I drop the bread
offering it, on the ground.
He glides down,
floating on grace,
and eagerly escorts it back to his perch.
I'm excited he accepts it,
after all,
crows always remember.
I sit and admire the crow,
enjoying his presence.
He then returns to me,
I feel accepted as a friend.
He is confident enough
to be within reach.
He stands next to me, content.
But I have no more bread.
Surely he will pluck out my eyes
in search of food.
I cower and cry
under the still, silent crow,
not wanting to shoo him away,
but unable to be next to him.

He leaves me, and flies away.

XIII.

Your words wreck me.
They make me some ancient
castle ruins.
War, wind, rain,
erosion for centuries
experienced
in seconds.

XIV.

I'm going back to my room
to eat
circle bread and Nutella.

* * *

XV.

My brow drips sweat
My legs groan
My back is weighted
My body,
has nothing left
to give.

I plead with it anyway.

Please, old friend,
just once more.

XVI.

Sometimes
I wish I could say
with all sincerity
and confidence
Let's go home

Where is it?
What is it?
What does it look like?
Does it have
a taste?

Is it people?
If so
I have left home
home
has left me

Are the trails
the dirt
the asphalt
where I walk,
home?

* * *

XVII.

A few months
and never again
could never hurt me.
My heart is protected,
it grew in a steel
coffin with wings.

* * *

XVIII.

My companions on that day
were solitude
and my frozen breath
Following packed down
steps
of wayfarers past
I scramble up
still Falling Waters
Rivers are frozen
in time
Fallen trees make
No sound
When dampened by falling snow
The forest was painted perfectly
But beauty
is not what drove me
that day

I was seeking
pain
release
limits
peace.
To be alone
is to get closer
to find.
I was completely alone,
too close to
finding.

I was exposed
on that frigid ridge.
Comforted by wind
and ice.
My clothes were ice
my beard snow.
Only grey clouds to warm me.

To push farther
is to get closer
to find.
Eroded by wind
I walk
I stumble
closer to finding.
I trek along the knife's edge
unknown to the world below.
Unable to stop,
my head dims
my vision spins
my legs shake.
I am pierced by air
soaked by snow.
The grey
unforgiving weather,
with spears of wind and daggers of ice,
matches my mind.
The storm is consistent
powerful
isolating,
I was alone in it.
My mind and legs
shaking
'It's ok

Lay down
Sleep
It can be over'
I might have found it.
My thoughts
are not my own.
I escaped in prayer,
my own, and of another.

The trees and still water
welcome me back,
the sun greets me.
I drive away
following the trail 93.
I look up at my
pain
release
limits
peace
Tears from my heart and mind
finally reach my eyes.

I found it
I have been conquered.

XIX.

The day my faith
was uprooted
was the day
it became intellectual

※ ※ ※

XX.

I've heard a voice
Telling me I am loved
I am protected
You are my son
In whom I am well pleased
Wishful thinking?
I want
to be wanted
Am I controlled by feeling?
Or comforted by my Father?

* * *

XXI.

From the beginning
God spoke
to create to teach
to guide to love.
He spoke to men of God
and to men of wickedness
and to sons and daughters.
He spoke through fire,
winds, thunder, clouds,
a quiet voice,
miracles, signs.
Even through a human voice
He spoke.

How does He speak to me?
Can I hear Him?
Is the rustling of the leaves,
and the mist on the lake in the morning,
His 'I love you'?
Is the quiet deer in the forest palace
staring at me
His 'I see you'?
Is the blueish green haze
of the mountains
His 'I am here'?
Or are all these simply
the emotions and thoughts
of my human mind?

Are the circumstances, the randomness of life
the coincidence, the chance encounters,
seeds planted,
His 'come this way'?
How can I know
if the desires of my heart and mind,
are planted by God?
Or a product,
a fabrication,
of my broken
fallen human mind.

* * *

XXII.

Blinding darkness
Chained freefall
Claustrophobic void
Frigid burns
Deafening silence
Suffocating breath

Perceiving, all of the nothing
Bound, to a bottomless pit
Crushed, by emptiness
Scorched, by the Cold Shoulder
Screaming, with no noise
Choking, on air

God is light
The truth will set you free
I am with you always
God is a consuming fire
My sheep hear my voice
The breath of the Almighty gives me life

But what if I'm wrong.

XXIII.

Do you still feel?
Do you still weep?
Is there an expiration date
on your pain?
Was it 33 AD?

I cannot ask
if you know my limp, my
broken spirit.
You know the moment the leaf
will fall.
But I will ask,
does it move you?
Do you wince at my struggle?

I've only heard my own tears.
Maybe yours ran dry.

* * *

XXIV.

I sit quiet in the circle,
my eyes are the only ones open.
I have an abundance of thoughts
and nothing to share.
If I wanted to share,
the words would definitely go missing.
I think the phone line is cut,
deadpan ringing inhabits my head.
Their words fall on human ears,
that much I know.
But do the words bounce off the ceiling?
Are they simply echoed back,
a pitiful form of self comfort?
Or do they have the power to break through?
To ascend past the atmosphere,
on the other side of the stars?
Do they carry enough power to reach celestial ears?
Or better, to provoke celestial tears?

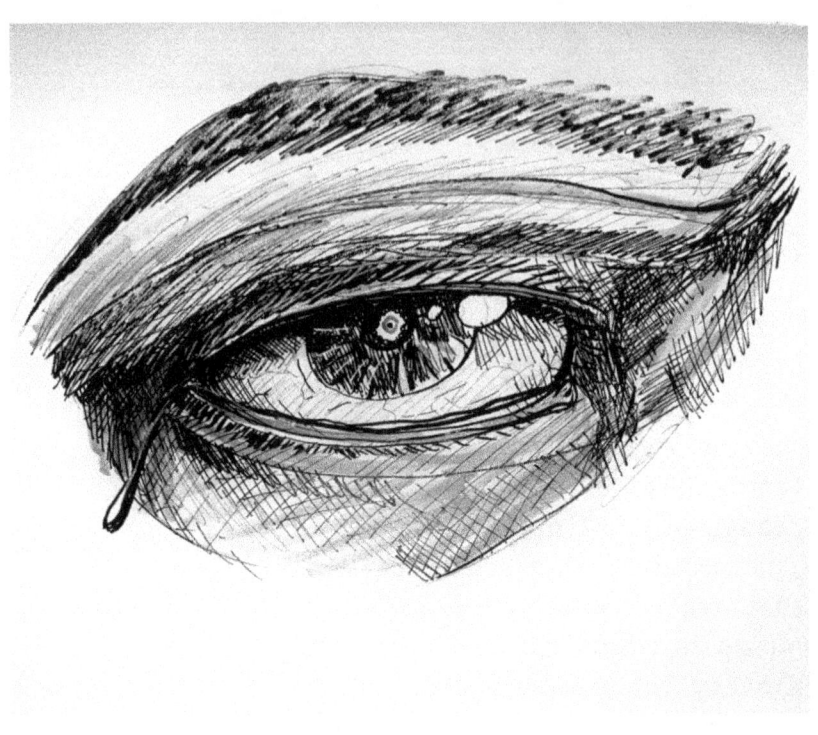

XXV.

I search for answers
and for comfort,
for peace, and intense feeling,
for emotion, and numbness,
I search for sleep, and the will
to stay awake.
I search for God,
and a hiding place from Him

I find it all
for a moment.

My eyes open
I am Jack's self-loathing
and regret.
My body pleads with my mind
My mind pleads with God.

Please
no more.

* * *

XXVI

I sit when others stand.
I am silent when others sing.
I find despair where others find hope.
I am condemned when others are free.
I have opinions while others have convictions.

Is peace a gift,
when earned by faith?
Exhibiting turmoil is unbelief,
unfaithfulness,
do you not have peace?

* * *

XXVII.

He hears the birds
calling through the first mist
waiting for the forest to respond.
He hears the rabbit
crying in the night
alone, frightened.
He hears the wolf
hunting, protecting,
howling at the departing moon.
He hears the fish
swimming up the stream
praising Him with their movement.
They all know Him.
They are connected to Him.
There is no mystery.
They do not doubt
or question their creator.

They don't understand their privilege,
I envy them.

Have I cut off my ears?
Have I sold them to another?
Or my eyes?
Are they lost to me?
Have I given up
my direct line to Him?
What must I do
to restore my wild

natural connection to
the Creator?
He hears them
running
grazing
climbing
living
loving
as they worship.

They do not understand their privilege.

XXVIII.

Is God watching me
from above?
Or
is He here with me,
walking alongside?

Does my wrestling and searching
frustrate Him from afar?
Or
does my pain and confusion
grieve Him, do my tears fall at His feet?

Does he know I search for Him,
in the wrong places?
Or
are you pleased with how far I go
to find you?

XXIX.

Do you have dreams
with hands made of vapor?
They make it impossible to save the little girl
sinking into the earth.
Do you have dreams
with feet made of lead?
They make it hard to catch the killer
before he reaches your family.
Do you have dreams
with a cold, distant God?
It makes it painful
to listen to songs of praise
sung by so many on a Sunday night.

* * *

XXX.

If you're so big
wrap me in your love
If you're so merciful
take away my shame
If you are the comforter,
comfort her
If you are so powerful
take over my life
If you love me so much
show me.

I don't think you will,
will you hold it against me?
Do I do the work?
Or will you be the
big
merciful
all powerful
God?

Prove yourself

* * *

XXXI.

Who has a greater faith?
The child,
innocent
pure
simple
accepting his gift?
Or the young man,
searching
wrestling
doubting
trying to find the truth?

* * *

XXXII.

I see it,
the landscape, the Beauty
from my dreams.
A mountain
strong, peaceful
a refuge.
The mountain,
seemingly one with the trees,
gracefully speaking,
dancing with the wind and birds.
How do they always
know the song?
Twin lakes,
source of peace, of life.
Reflecting the light of the sun,
the most beautiful
shades of green
and golden brown.
Surely this,
a reflection of Eden,
is how I am blessed.

XXXIII. MY MOST PRECIOUS DAUGHTER

He
the One in the chaos
before time
the One who carved
the cosmos
and stretches them
He
the One who shaped
the earth, the ranges of mountains
dug the oceans
with His hands
He
the One who has counted
every atom in your body
and holds them
in His Love
He
the One who gave
himself to save
you
Just to save you
his most precious
daughter

He does not allow
you
to speak.
Be Silent

* * *

XXXIV.

Time's almost up
I soak in the golden
sea
and your head
on my shoulder

I have to leave
my paradise
behind
not the island
but half my soul

My shirt is damp
not from ocean
spray
but the mourning
from our hearts

XXXV.

I am greeted by light,
the sun pouring in through the windows
facing east.
The only thing on my schedule,
and my to-do list,
is to be with you.

There you are next to me,
closed eyes punctuate the beauty
of your face.
I am anchored by your warmth and peace.
I could never leave.
I admire you and bask in your light.

* * *

XXXVI.

I'm terrified you are
my imagination.
That I will continue to go to sleep
longing for your smile,
your touch,
and continue to wake up
without it.
Endlessly hoping
with no reward.

* * *

XXXVII.

When I reunite with
others,
I want to sing, laugh.

But you're different.

When I reunite with
you,
I can at long last, breathe.

* * *

XXXVIII.

The sun finally has
dominion
over the trees, and sky,
the fields, and hills.
The birds are awakened
and singing their songs
of joy, and warmth,
and freedom.
The trees are soaked
with light, and warmth,
and fresh air.
And I am soaking it all in.
I sit among the trees
with the old bearded poet.
He tells me of the lands
of freedom, and expression,
and love.
He teaches me of the love
felt between brothers.
I am warmed by his words
like from the scarce
winter sun
peering through the clouds
of my mind.
I ask the old man a question
but he dare not break
from his song
of the manly love of comrades.

XXXIX.

If mountain paths
could tell their tales
I would sit and listen,
absorbing stories of
travelers past.
Footprints would tell me
their direction,
where they came from.
The trails would tell me
second hand wisdom
from grey haired hikers.
The trees would share
tales of the woodland creatures.
I would sit and listen,
waiting for the words pouring out
like syrup.
I thank them for their stories,
and I continue forward,
trying to catch up
to the grey haired hikers.

XL.

I grew up in mountains
separated by an ocean
I Dolomiti hidden behind
the Whites
This is where Eden is
Where God planted my
Tree of Life
Where I am sent visions
on hooves
and messages on wings

I receive safe passage
on ridges and planes
13 countries and counting
Will I forever
be a stranger to all?
Known only by
my Ezer
my kindred spirit
singing mountain sounds

I seek the creator of this world
Where is He
in this cosmic temple?
This trail has 24
brothers
I have a bearing
to set me straight
but was my knife

too close to the needle?
I know God made
me:
Bagger of peaks
Brother, oldest of three
Embrace of change
Shoulderer of burdens
Writer of longing
Lover of my One
Receiver of grace
Inheritor of sonship

XLI.

Preparing to complete its silent, invisible harvest, the figure approaches, clothed in shadow as a cloak.

The man's head turns slightly, his body follows,
"Good evening"

The figure stops, then starts again slowly.

"Come join me, you can catch it still."

The figure sits with some distance, facing the sun setting over the valley,
"I have a job to do."

"I know. I thought maybe the view would stall you."

The figure doesn't turn to face the man, if it had eyebrows they would have been furrowed.
"How can you see me?"

The old man shrugs, and lets out a small chuckle, his gaze still fixed over the valley.
"Not what you expected your first time to be like, huh?"

"No, but it doesn't matter if you see me or not, it's too late, I'm taking you."

"Yes I know, if it's all the same to you though, I'd like to see the end of the sunset."

"As you wish." The figure sits in silence for a few moments, "Have you ever seen one before?"

"I couldn't count how many times I've watched the fading orange sky."

"Is it worth it?"

The man nods,
"Every time."

"Can I ask another question? I never thought I'd be able to talk to you."

"Of course."

The figure pauses, choosing its words carefully,
"Are you ready to die?"

"Well, the sun is still here, so no."

"That's not what I meant, was your...pre-death... enjoyable?"

"You mean my life? Sometimes it was, but I think the answer you're looking for is: Yes, I lived a good life. I am ready in that sense."

"What made it so? What marks a good, 'life', as you call it? They all culminate to death, no matter what."

The man finally turned toward the figure, looking at where its face would be, although briefly before returning his gaze pensively over The Valley. He waited a few moments before speaking.
"I think all the sunsets have something to do with it, and definitely the sunrises. I had good friends, they understood me, at least as well as they could, and I did my best to understand them. I loved, even when I was bad at it, but maybe most importantly, I was loved."

"That sounds like it was nice for you."

"It was, not always though. It was hard a lot of the time, but it was the life I was given, and I did my best to live it fully."

"I see, so you feel sorrow about what I have to do?"

"It's not as simple as that, many parts of my life were beautiful, and I saw and experienced much of the good it had to offer. But I am old now, I've ran my race and fought many battles, inside and out. And I've been incredibly lonely since my Heart left."

"Your heart is still beating in your flesh; you make no sense."

"No, she was the person that mattered most to me. We helped each other through ups and downs, cried together, laughed together, we did it all. We lived for each other, and she knew me like no one else. That is why I'm ready."

"Are the rest of you like this? So talkative?"

"You don't want to hear their stories?"

The figure turns toward the man,
"No, I do, but I don't like this confusion of words and mixed round about answers. Death is the course for everything, all things run towards its embrace, there is no point in feeling a certain way about it."

"But the confusion is fun, and beautiful, like being rained on when the sun is shining, or seeing the moon in the daytime. This confusion and mess is life and it is what embraced me for better or worse."

The figure nodded slowly,

"It does sound nice, I mean, beautiful, what you had."

"Thank you," the old man smiled.

"It's time now, we must go."

But they didn't go quite yet, the two continued sitting, drinking in the dying of the light, not knowing exactly what would come next.

www.ingramcontent.com/pod-product-compliance
Lightning Source LLC
Chambersburg PA
CBHW050916160426
43194CB00011B/2435